Thirteen Candles

Mary Hooper

Illustrated by Maureen Gray

A & C Black • London

Chapter One

My thirteenth birthday, 23rd July, was a wonderful day.
There were balloons and "Happy Birthday, Julia!" banners
all over the wall in the dining room. I spent the day with
my mum, dad, and best friend Emma.

Mum had some soppy idea about having a proper, sit-down dinner for
my birthday party. Apart from that, everything was perfect.

As I said, it was a perfect day. So why was there a funny knot in my tummy? Why was there a strange shivery tingle going up and down my spine?

I tried my best to ignore the feeling, but it wouldn't go away. Then in the afternoon, something really strange happened.

OK, Julia, brace yourself. Here comes the cake!

Time to blow out the candles and make a wish!

I grinned at Emma. She knew and I knew that there was only one real wish – for Simon Elkins to ask me out.

Mum put the cake on the table – a proper birthday cake with silver decorations, pink and white icing and candles. Emma and I had already gone through the ordeal of egg and cress sandwiches, sausage rolls and jelly and ice cream. Now I had to endure the full birthday girl bit and sit squirming while they sang "Happy Birthday".

Are you ready, Bill?

7

Ready to roll!

The camera was a recent purchase, bought especially to film my birthday and our coming summer holiday.

Sorry about this.

Dad turned out the lights, and Mum carefully lit the 13 birthday candles.

Right, love! All set. Look at the camera and get ready to blow.

The heat from the candles was making my cheeks warm.
OK, I thought, birthday cakes are for kids. But if I'm
having a cake, I might as well have the wish that goes
with it. Thinking of a wish in my mind, I took a deep
breath…

Suddenly, right in front of my eyes, the flames on the candles went out. But I hadn't even blown on them.

As Mum, Dad and Emma started to sing, I stared at the candles, stunned.

Happy Birthday to you...

Maybe they were trick candles, a special sort that all went out together. It would be typical of my family to buy trick candles.

Happy Birthday to you...

But I knew they weren't. Mum had used some out of the same box for Dad's birthday earlier this year. I'd bought them myself. Then how did they go out by themselves?

I frowned. How had it happened? A sudden gust of wind? No. It was a stuffy, airless day without a trace of a breeze.

Happy Birthday, dear Julia...

What, then? Had Emma blown them out for me as a joke? Not that, either. The candles streamed their little blue-orange flames away from me before they went out.

As if the person who'd blown them had been standing right behind me.

Happy Birthday to you!

The tingle ran right down my spine again, and I shivered.

Mum reached for the cake to begin cutting it.

What's up, honey? You look like you've seen a ghost.

13

Later, Dad filmed me and Emma getting ready to go out.
He added some embarrassing commentary.

Here's my gorgeous daughter and her lovely friend getting ready to hit the town.

Oh, Dad, turn that thing off!

Finally, Emma and I managed to escape. We went to the local hangout, just in case there was anyone there worth talking with.

There wasn't. It seemed that anyone interesting (by that I mean Simon Elkins or Richard James) had gone away for the weekend. So, it didn't look as if I was going to get my birthday wish – at least not today.

When we got back, Dad and Mum were waiting to watch the film of my birthday.

Take your seats, girls! Ice cream will be served during the interval.

Dads!

Emma and I pulled faces at each other; my one consolation was that her dad's nearly as bad as mine. We sat on the floor, lolling one each side of a squashy cushion, while Dad started the film.

The film started in the morning with "Here's the birthday girl emerging from the duvet!"…

…and carried on through the "highlights" of the day.

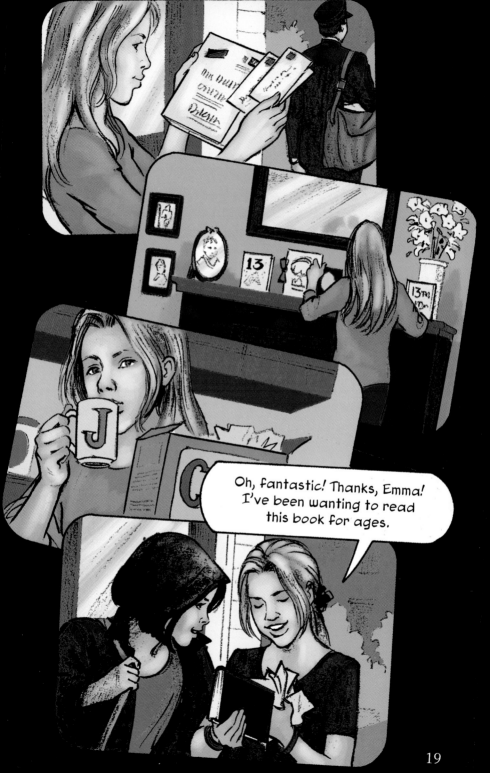

It was all pretty boring stuff until we got to the part with the birthday cake and candles. Then the film stopped being boring and got puzzling and weird and mysterious and scary as well.

I watched myself looking at the camera and saw myself breathe in. But then I saw a shadow behind me, a dark, hazy shape leaning forward, over my shoulder.

The film finally finished with a handwritten card.

I couldn't wait to escape. As soon as I could, I dragged Emma up to my room.

Did you see it?

Did you see that shady thing behind me?

Emma nodded.

What do you think it was?

I don't know. A spot on the film or something, I expect.

I shook my head.

No!
It was something else.
Something real. It blew
the candles out!

Emma looked at me in disbelief.

What do you mean?

Just what I said.
I didn't blow those candles out.
It did.

I nodded, and I was suddenly really scared. I shivered as a tingle went down my spine.

Chapter Two

I didn't sleep well that night. That's unusual for me. I normally drift off as soon as I close my eyes and don't budge until morning.

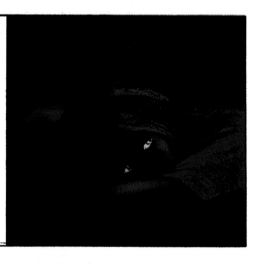

Instead, I kept having this dream – or nightmare. I was being followed by a shadow which disappeared every time I turned round to face it.

Several times I woke up and looked fearfully into the corners of my room, searching for shadows…

When morning finally came, Mum came in with a cup of tea. My sheets and covers, usually so smooth and untroubled, were all gnarled and twisted around.

Are you all right? It looks like you've been having a fight with someone.

I got dressed and went downstairs to have breakfast. While I chomped on my cornflakes, I glanced at Mum's magazine. It was open to the astrology page.

Hmm. Let's see what the stars have in store for me.

"If your birthday is 23rd July, you're in danger..."

I couldn't take another bite.

I'm in danger! I knew it!

I'd felt weird all day yesterday, then those spooky things had happened, and then there had been the nightmares. Together, they foretold something dreadful...

I put down the spoon and turned the magazine round so I could read the whole piece.

LEO
22nd July – 22nd August

If your birthday is 23rd July, you're in danger of getting everything you want.

I breathed again and took another mouthful of cereal.
Julia, you're getting crazy in your old age, I thought to myself.

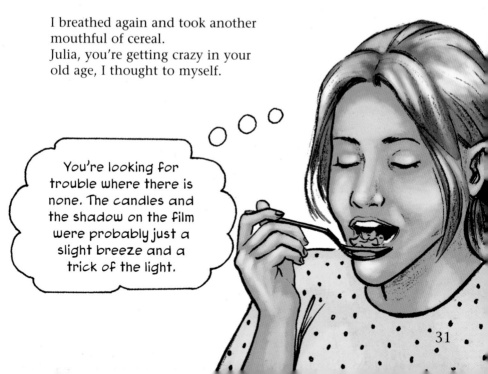

You're looking for trouble where there is none. The candles and the shadow on the film were probably just a slight breeze and a trick of the light.

31

Emma came over later, and we decided to go into town and do some shopping. Pretty soon we were laughing about the goings-on of the day before.

33

Emma grinned and nudged me.

What's it worth not to tell Simon what sort of party you had?

You dare!

I'd almost forgotten the things that had happened – except the words "you're in danger" kept repeating themselves over and over in rhythm with my footsteps as we walked along. I didn't say anything to Emma, though, I knew she'd just think I was being silly.

When we got home, Dad was filming again. He'd borrowed the neighbour's dog, and he was trying to film him doing tricks. I think he was hoping the dog would do something silly. Then he could send the film in to TV and maybe win some money.

When Emma and I turned up, he made us act out a crazy scene for him.

It's just a bit of fun. I want you to take Rover here for a walk, and I'll film you going up the road.

Then what?

Once Mr Film Producer of the Year had finished, we went to Emma's house for something to eat. When we got back, Dad wanted us to sit and watch the movie he'd made.

Roll up! Roll up! I think you're going to like this one.

Dutifully, we went into the sitting room and sat down in front of the TV.

When it came to the bit where I was walking down the road with Emma, I couldn't believe what I saw.

It's there again, behind me! Look! The shadow!

It's only your dad's technique. It's bound to be a bit shaky and out of focus while he's learning.

Do you mind? I'm a professional!

No! I don't mean that; I don't mean it's just a bit fuzzy. There's a shape right behind me, tracking my footsteps. You can see it, can't you, Emma?

Emma nodded slowly, staring at the screen.

Yeah, same height as you. Same hair. Same size.

Emma leaned closer to the screen to get a better look.

No, it's not. It's like you have someone standing behind you. Your double.

Just as she said that, two things happened; the film came to an end, and Mum dropped the cup of tea she was holding.

We all looked at each other. Then, Mum dashed out of the room, as if she was going to burst into tears.

What was that all about?

Your Mum's just upset because... because that's her best cup she's broken.

I looked at Dad hard. It couldn't have been that because it was a really old cup, not her best china at all. No, something else had upset her. And it was something to do with that shadow...

Chapter Three

Something was definitely wrong. Since my birthday, my life had changed. Mum seemed different, quieter and preoccupied. Several times, I caught her staring into space like something was on her mind.

What's up, Mum? You're being really quiet.

What? Me? Don't be silly. You're imagining things.

I knew I wasn't imagining things, though. The shivery, frightened feeling that had started on my birthday stayed with me. Often at night, I'd lay awake with the words "You're in danger" pounding through my head.

Once, just as the clock was striking three, I suddenly awoke. I sat up in bed, certain that there was someone in the room. Certain Shadow was there.

Who's there?

What do you want?

I stared towards the window, where a street light shone dimly through my blind. A shape was outlined there; a blurry mass silhouetted against the light.

Shadow seemed to take a step towards me, arms outstretched.

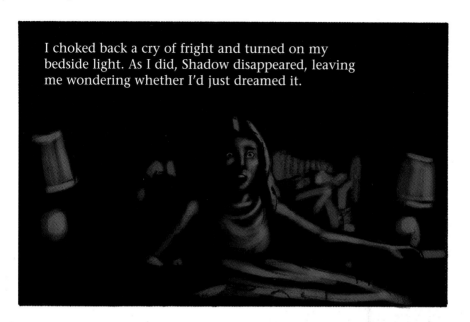

I choked back a cry of fright and turned on my bedside light. As I did, Shadow disappeared, leaving me wondering whether I'd just dreamed it.

I couldn't go back to sleep. Instead, I left the light on and read until the sun came up.

I began to want to get away from the house. A couple of nights I stayed over at Emma's, and I found it much easier to sleep there.

I started looking forward to going away on holiday. It wasn't going to happen until the end of August, though, which seemed like years away.

So I was pleased when Dad said we were going to the seaside for a long weekend.

Can Emma come too?

Sure, why not?

I wasn't so pleased when we got there and it rained for two days. Emma and I just sat around watching the rain running down the windows.

If this raindrop gets to the bottom first, then Simon's going to ask me out before we go back to school.

No. If this raindrop gets there first, then Richard's going to ask me.

Only once did I bring up the subject of Shadow, but Emma didn't want to talk about it.

You remember that strange thing that happened on my birthday...

The only strange thing that happened on your birthday was being made to sit down and eat jelly and ice cream.

On the day we were going home, the wind stopped and the sun came out.

Of course, Dad got out his camcorder.

OK, girls, the sun's shining. Let's play some volleyball on the beach!

He packed the camcorder into a bag and headed for the door.

I'll get out of practice with this if I'm not careful.

Emma and I put on our shorts and compared tans.

I ran over to get it back. The cliff had cast large shadows on the beach and, as I went into the shade, the sand was suddenly cold under my feet. Without the warmth of the sun, I shivered, half from cold and half from, well, that feeling again. That frightened, scary feeling that someone was close to me, watching me all the time.

I paused for a moment. You're crazy, I told myself. Don't be such a drip!

I took a step towards the ball. Then I heard a strange rumbling coming from above.

I stayed frozen to the spot and suddenly I felt – and saw – Shadow.

It seemed to come towards me from out of the cliff, growing deeper and denser as it did so.

You're in danger!

I wanted to scream but there wasn't time. Shadow just literally shoved me off my feet, throwing me sideways so that I landed in a heap of sand.

I heard Emma and Dad shout something – and then there was an almighty crashing noise and I automatically curled up and felt myself being hit by a shower of small stones.

When I opened my eyes, Dad, Mum and Emma were all racing towards me.

Are you all right?

Oh, Julia!

It was a moment before I realised what had happened: a chunk of the cliff had fallen exactly where I'd been standing – I could see a piece of the beach ball there to prove it. If Shadow hadn't shoved me out of the way, I'd have been killed...

Chapter Four

Sun or no sun, none of us could relax or enjoy the day now. Dad called the police and went to see the coastguard about the falling rocks, and then we drove straight home.

During the journey, I thought things over. I didn't know what to think. Had I just dreamed up Shadow? If I had, it was a lucky dream – one which had saved my life. Maybe Dad's film would give me an answer.

As soon as we got home, I asked Dad if we could see the film.

What for?

I didn't film very much.

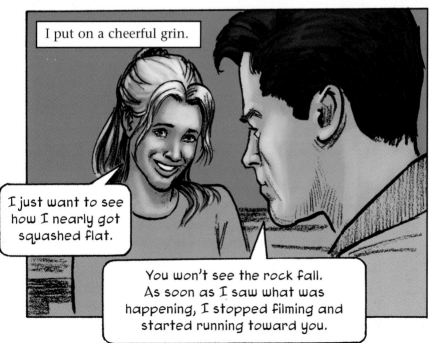

I put on a cheerful grin.

I just want to see how I nearly got squashed flat.

You won't see the rock fall. As soon as I saw what was happening, I stopped filming and started running toward you.

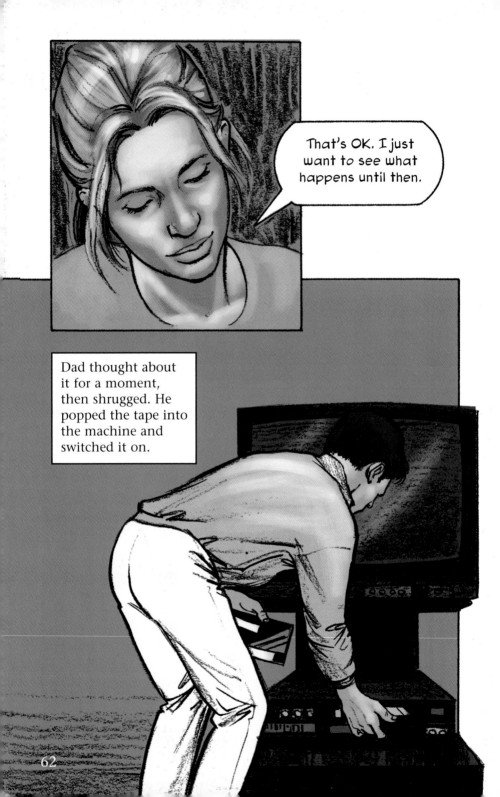

That's OK. I just want to see what happens until then.

Dad thought about it for a moment, then shrugged. He popped the tape into the machine and switched it on.

The film began with Emma and me coming down
the cliff steps toward Mum and Dad on the beach.

It went blank for a second, then started again with us
playing with the ball, knocking it backwards and forwards
over the windbreak and calling to each other.

Then Emma punched the ball towards the cliff, and it went out of the camera shot.

I watched myself run off to fetch it. Reaching the shade, I hesitated for a moment.

A split-second later, we all gasped. We watched in disbelief as the shape of a person appeared out of nowhere and pushed me out of danger.

Then it all went blurred and blacked out because Dad had

No one said anything for a moment. Then I turned to face them.

There! You all saw that, didn't you? You saw Shadow come out of nowhere. You can't say I'm imagining it now.

It was just like the shadow behind you on the other film.

It saved my life. It pushed me out of the way of the rockfall.

I was completely bewildered. OK, so I'd nearly had a nasty accident, but I was all right now. So why were they both looking at each other in that peculiar way? Why was Mum crying? Then Dad spoke.

71

Joy and Julia. You were like two peas in a pod.

I gazed at them in disbelief. Emma spoke for me.

What happened?

Joy died. She only lived for a day.

We were so upset, we couldn't bear to talk about it. We pretended to most people that there had only been one baby.

I took a deep breath, and I thought about how strange and how incredible it would have been to have had a twin.

So now...

So now, well, I never would have believed it if I hadn't seen it.

But now... maybe Joy wants to make her presence felt.

The realisation flooded through me.

Of course! She didn't like being forgotten. She wants to be part of the family!

Do you think so?

Yes!

Chapter Five

I didn't, though.
About four o'clock in
the morning, I got up
and went downstairs. I
wanted to see the films
again. Had Joy really
grown as I'd grown?
Was she really exactly
like me in every way
– apart from the fact
that I was alive and
she was dead.

The films were clear, bright, and normal – no shadow,
no double, no twin. I sat downstairs until the sun came
up, searching the films for a trace of her.

She's disappeared!

But there was none.

Maybe Joy just wanted to be recognised and acknowledged. And maybe what she'd done for me had been enough for her. But she was never going to be forgotten again now, and the memory of her would live on – I would make sure of that.

Maybe she'll appear again if I'm in danger.

Only time would tell...